DAVE WEBER (not his real name) knew he was in trouble. An underclassman at Stanford University, Dave, like many others, harbored ambitions of graduating and going on to success in Silicon Valley. But in February 2011, he received notice from Stanford that a female student had filed a sexual assault charge against him, alleging that a sexual encounter six weeks before had been, unbeknownst to Dave, nonconsensual.

How, one might ask, could someone unknowingly commit sexual assault? To Stanford, it was simple: both Dave and his accuser had been drinking. Stanford's policy at the time stated, "A person is legally incapable of giving consent ... if intoxicated by drugs or alcohol." This seemingly straightforward statement is far vaguer than it sounds, most importantly because it is not actually true. People who are merely intoxicated to some extent – in other words, people who have been drinking anything alcoholic at all – legally consent to sex all the time. California law, as with that of virtually every state, recognizes

[

this, specifying that when it comes to the lack of ability to consent to sex, "[i]t is not enough that the victim was intoxicated to some degree, or that the intoxication reduced the victim's sexual inhibitions." Even the most intense crusader against campus sexual assault would be hard-pressed to defend the idea that sexual activity after *any* amount of alcohol or drugs constitutes rape.

So Dave thought he had a reasonable chance at his hearing. The policy had obviously been carelessly drafted, and Stanford campus tribunals, like the criminal justice system, required that disciplinary charges be proved "beyond a reasonable doubt." Dave hired a lawyer and was able to gather witness statements and other evidence for his hearing that, he thought, would demonstrate that even though his accuser had been drinking, she wasn't too drunk to consent. He received more good news in March, when the local district attorney informed Dave's attorney that no criminal charges would be filed. His campus hearing was scheduled for Apr. 11, 2011.

*OCR's letter would serve
as the starting whistle for
a new age of federal
intervention in academia.*

What Dave didn't know was that his hearing would come exactly one week too late, and that a fluke of scheduling would change the course of his life. Because on Apr. 4, 2011, the U.S. Department of Education's Office for Civil Rights (OCR) issued a letter unlawfully mandating that the standard of proof in campus sexual misconduct cases be set at the lowest possible level: a "preponderance of the evidence," or a mere 50.01 percent likelihood of guilt. Stanford immediately applied this standard of proof to Dave, right in the middle of his case, leading to his "conviction" in a campus kangaroo court. As it turned out, this letter would serve as the starting whistle for a new age of federal intervention in academia –

an era that would see OCR's actions destroy the academic careers (and, in some cases, the lives) of countless students like Dave accused of sexual misconduct, prompt administrators at nearly every American college and university to rush headlong toward censorship and grossly unfair treatment of students, and stand as one of the most unrepentant abuses of the regulatory system in recent times. All in the name of a 1972 law called Title IX.

WHAT IS TITLE IX AND WHERE DID IT COME FROM?

Title IX is the primary federal law intended to prohibit sex discrimination in federally funded education programs. The operative part of the law (which is followed by myriad exceptions) is a mere 37 words long:

> *No person in the United States shall, on the basis of sex, be excluded from participation in, be denied the benefits of, or be subjected to discrimination under any education program or activity receiving Federal financial assistance.*

Since federal funding includes ordinary grants to schools or school districts as well as student-directed funds such as Pell grants and Stafford loans, Title IX applies to all public schools, from the K–12 level all the way through graduate school, as well as to the overwhelming majority of private universities in the United States. The number of private universities that do not at least accept federal student loans may well be in the single digits. Since losing such funding would generally be a death sentence for all but the richest schools, Title IX and its interpretations have become the main cudgel with which federal bureaucrats beat colleges and universities into submission to their policy objectives. Compared to that threat, the once-substantial influence that the First Amendment and other constitutional principles had on private university policies has been vastly reduced.

Until quite recently, when most people thought of Title IX, it was generally in the context of college athletics. It is, most notoriously, the reason many colleges have more women's NCAA sports than men's. Because fielding a football team requires many substantial athletic scholarships, and because the current interpretation of Title IX effectively requires schools to provide athletic scholarships for men and women in numbers proportionate to their percentage of all students, female students can often receive athletic scholarships for nonrevenue sports like rowing or lacrosse when men cannot. Women have outnumbered men in college since 1979 and currently make up 57 percent of undergraduates (higher at some schools), so the seemingly easier access to scholarships for women has long been controversial.

Indeed, early discussions of Title IX in the press focused overwhelmingly on its impact on college athletics, as a search of the *New York Times* archive from the first half of the 1970s indicates. But it wasn't long before activists for women's issues found in the law a tool for combating a number of other social ills, starting with sexual harassment.

* * *

In the 1977 case of *Alexander v. Yale*, using a framework developed by then Yale law student (and later famed feminist activist and antiporn crusader) Catharine MacKinnon, a federal court found that colleges could be liable under Title IX not just for allowing overt discrimination but also for not responding to allegations of sexual harassment by professors. In that case, the issue that survived the preliminary pleadings was an allegedly straightforward offer by a professor to give student-plaintiff Pamela Price an *A* in exchange for sex. Price ultimately failed to prove at trial that the sexual proposition ever occurred, but the precedent was set: sexual harassment could now be considered discrimination and was thus within the province of Title IX.

The kind of harassment allegedly experienced by Pamela Price is called "quid pro quo" harassment. It was then, and is now, universally recognized as morally wrong behavior (even if the law had not yet caught up to that conception). It's also what most people think of when they think of sexual harassment. But at around the same time, a new kind of sexual harassment was beginning to be recognized by courts and government agencies: "hostile environment" sexual harassment. In 1980, the Equal Employment Opportunity Commission (EEOC), which administers the law known as Title VII banning sex discrimination in employment, passed regulations defining this new kind of sexual harassment as sexually discriminatory "conduct [that] has the purpose or effect of unreasonably interfering with an individual's work performance or creating an intimidating, hostile, or offensive working environment."

Such conduct did not need to be intentional. It didn't even have to come from a specific person or be aimed at making people uncomfortable. For instance, if workers at a factory commonly posted nude centerfolds in their workspace, under the new standard, this would likely create a hostile environment and therefore be considered sexual harassment even if there was no intent to make women uncomfortable and nobody was targeted.

As you might imagine, a standard of harassment that required neither intent nor a target struck many people as troublesome. The then chair of the EEOC, Eleanor Holmes Norton (who has since served 13 terms as the District of Columbia's representative in Congress), noted in the introduction to the new regulations that the EEOC had received a large number of comments pointing to the new hostile environment standard as the "most troublesome definition of what constitutes sexual harassment." She said, however, that the commission was convinced it was

Losing federal funding would generally be a death sentence for all but the richest schools.

"necessary." And in 1986, the Supreme Court ratified the EEOC's concept of "hostile environment" harassment, at least in the workplace. (Catharine MacKinnon was involved in that case as well, co-writing the brief for the plaintiff in *Meritor Savings Bank v. Vinson*.)

A Full-Employment Program for the Speech Police

If your workplace has a rule against dating other employees or your college prohibits instructors from dating students, the "hostile environment" standard is the reason. If your school or workplace tells you certain words are totally off-limits, this is why. The mandatory sexual harassment trainings that now feature in virtually every workplace – seminars that are run by an industry of amazingly well-paid "trainers" and are often mocked, frequently bizarre, and nearly always pretty awkward – are the direct result of the adoption of the idea of hostile environment sexual harassment. And the acceptance of the hostile environment doctrine by the Supreme

Court turned out to be the inflection point that would change Title IX into a flexible tool used by activists to address any number of perceived societal ills that could arguably be linked to sex or gender.

With the table set from a legal perspective, the explosion of "political correctness" onto the scene in the 1990s led both the government and college administrators to put teeth into this expanded conception of Title IX. (Not coincidentally, that decade also saw the birth of FIRE, the Foundation for Individual Rights in Education, of which I am executive director, in 1999.) In 1994, OCR launched an investigation into Santa Rosa Junior College in California after two female students complained about "anatomically explicit and sexually derogatory terms" used in comments about them posted on an online college forum. OCR's conclusion was that this created a hostile environment for the students and ordered the college to adopt a clearly unconstitutional rule that would punish speech protected by the First Amendment – a "speech

code." When the University of Massachu-
setts Amherst put in place a broad, unconstitutional speech code the following year,
Chancellor David K. Scott suggested that the
Department of Education now required it.

What would this mean in terms of administrators' attitudes toward free speech? The
short answer is that it has resulted in nearly
two decades of bad examples for college students of how to handle free speech in a free
society.

THE CURIOUS CASE OF PROFESSOR KIPNIS

Laura Kipnis is a film professor at Northwestern University, near Chicago. One might
think that a woman deemed a "provocative
feminist" by the *Nation*, a leading liberal mag-
azine, would have little trouble under a regime
designed to put an end to sex discrimination
on campus. But Kipnis quickly found out
that, thanks to Title IX, expressing a controversial opinion is anything but safe on today's
campuses.

Kipnis's "offense" was writing an article for the *Chronicle of Higher Education* (the primary trade publication for college faculty and administrators) titled "Sexual Paranoia Strikes Academe." The February 2015 article took as its launching point Northwestern's recent ban on faculty–student romantic or sexual relationships, relationships that, in earlier decades, were quite common. Kipnis wrote critically about the increasing regulation of sexual expression and behavior on campus. Observing that "students' sense of vulnerability is skyrocketing," Kipnis pointed out problems with various policies, including the university's sexual harassment policy, which banned "inappropriate jokes," remarking, "I'd always thought inappropriateness was pretty much the definition of humor – I believe Freud would agree."

Kipnis also related several other vignettes of faculty–student sexual interactions – including the facts of a well-known and widely publicized case of alleged sexual harassment of a student by a philosophy professor – and the various campus reactions to them. She concluded, "The new codes sweeping American campuses aren't just a striking abridgment of everyone's freedom, they're also intellectually embarrassing. Sexual paranoia reigns; students are trauma cases waiting to happen. If you wanted to produce a pacified, cowering citizenry, this would be the method. And in that sense, we're all the victims."

As if to prove her point, the reaction to this newspaper article was paranoid, swift, and over the top. Students held protests, dragging mattresses and pillows to the administration building, and filed a petition demanding that the university president officially condemn the article. Soon after, Kipnis was informed by Northwestern's Title IX office that two complaints had been filed against her for violating Title IX with her newspaper article and a subsequent single tweet. Among the charges were that Kipnis had created a "chilling effect" on reports of sexual harassment, that Kipnis had "retaliated" against a student she mentioned (though not by name and in an ancillary fashion) in her article, and, of course, that she had created a "hostile environment."

There's no doubt that a hostile environment existed at Northwestern – for Professor Kipnis. She asked if she could have an attorney present during the investigation. This was denied, although she was allowed a "support person." She asked to be given the specific charges against her in writing. This, too, was denied. Instead, two out-of-town attorneys would be assigned to investigate her, and they would tell her the charges immediately before questioning her about them. She finally agreed to a Skype session with the lawyers, which she was denied permission to record. Professor

Female students can often receive athletic scholarships for nonrevenue sports like rowing or lacrosse when men cannot.

Kipnis never saw any of the evidence against her. Her "support person," who talked in general terms about the case in front of the faculty senate, was slapped with a Title IX complaint for doing so and banned from continuing to be Kipnis's official support person.

With the 60-day "deadline" for making a decision on her case having already passed, Professor Kipnis did the smartest thing she could have done – she blew the whistle on what was happening to her in a second essay in the *Chronicle of Higher Education*: "My Title IX Inquisition." It was only fair. Whereas Professor Kipnis had been asked to keep the proceedings confidential, a student claiming to have highly detailed knowledge of unnamed "factual inaccuracies" in her original article had taken to the pages of the *Huffington Post* to bash her. And as the investigation dragged on with no end in sight, Kipnis's follow-up article had a rapid and profound effect: two days after it was published, Kipnis was informed that she was cleared of all charges.

* * *

POWER DIFFERENTIALS AND
PEER HARASSMENT

The case against Professor Kipnis, absurd though it was, rested in part on the premise that a professor like Laura Kipnis is a powerful person on campus compared to a student. People are naturally more suspicious of events that can be framed as an abuse of power, and the concept of power differentials is critical to the idea of quid pro quo harassment – after all, you cannot offer someone a promotion in exchange for sex if you have no promotion to give. But most interactions on campuses are among students, who are peers, not between students and professors. In 1999, the Supreme Court took up the issue of the hostile environment doctrine at school and among students in the case of *Davis v. Monroe County Board of Education.* Attorneys for Georgia fifth-grader LaShonda Davis argued that the school district's "deliberate indifference" to the sexual harassment of Davis by a fellow student violated Title IX by allowing a hostile environment to be created that effectively deprived Davis of an education.

The facts alleged in *Davis* were ugly, especially given the elementary school context. According to the complaint, a student referred to as G.F. "attempted to touch LaShonda's breasts and genital area and made vulgar statements such as 'I want to get in bed with you' and 'I want to feel your boobs.'" Such incidents happened repeatedly over a span of about five months, but the school did nothing effective to stop the behavior until G.F. was ultimately charged with (and pled guilty to) sexual battery.

At issue in the case was the question of whether Title IX applied only to discrimination (including sexual harassment) by the school and its employees, or whether schools could also be held liable for hostile environments created by students, over whom they had far less control. The decision split the Court's liberals and conservatives, with Justice O'Connor joining the liberals in a 5–4 decision that, yes, schools could be liable under Title IX for deliberate indifference to student behavior that created a hostile environment. Schools were now officially on the hook for policing sexual behavior taking place solely among students.

However, the Court went to some pains to limit the scenarios in which a school could be held liable for allowing the creation of a hostile environment – limits much tighter than those permitted in the employment context. At least some degree of free expression is fundamental to the academic enterprise, and schools don't have nearly the control over students that employers have over employees. Therefore, under *Davis*, if schools are to be held responsible for violating Title IX in this context, they must be "deliberately indifferent to sexual harassment, of which they have actual knowledge, that is so severe, pervasive, and objectively offensive that it can be said to deprive the victims of access to the educational opportunities or benefits provided by the school."

It didn't take long at all for OCR to seize

on *Davis* to start more closely regulating schools under the aegis of Title IX. On Jan. 19, 2001 – the very last day of the Bill Clinton

---

Colleges became liable under Title IX not just for allowing overt discrimination but also for not responding to allegations of sexual harassment.

---

administration – OCR released a "Revised Sexual Harassment Guidance" document that took advantage of the *Davis* decision to lay out 23 pages of regulations (not counting a whopping 119 footnotes) governing how schools must henceforth treat sexual harassment allegations. Given this regulation's publication on the last day of Clinton's term, one can safely assume that OCR was concerned that the incoming George W. Bush administration would have scrapped the regulation and started over instead of issuing it.

But it *was* sneaked in under the wire, and it *did* go into effect. What could go wrong?

Five Conduct Charges for a Four-Word Joke

Sarah Emerson (not her real name) was a sophomore at the University of Oregon in Eugene. At around 9 P.M. on June 9, 2014 – the first evening of Oregon's week of final exams – Sarah was taking a break and looking out the window of her dormitory. Seeing a man and woman below and figuring, correctly, that they were romantically involved, she jokingly yelled, "I hit it first!" (The phrase is a euphemism for "I had sex with him/her first" or "I hooked up with him/her first," and had been popularized the previous year in a song by R&B singer Ray J.) Sarah did not know either party and obviously meant it as a joke, but the woman below didn't think it was funny, responding, "Fuck you, bitch!" Not satisfied with simply yelling back, the couple marched into Sarah's dorm, identified her by figuring out which window belonged to her, and, in the company of a resident assistant, stormed upstairs to demand an apology. Sarah immediately apologized as demanded, adding that it was a joke and she meant no offense.

In a sane world, that would have been the end of the matter. But the Title IX–driven pressure to police, investigate, and crack down on every reported offense on campus, no matter how frivolous, has resulted in a campus culture that is anything but sane. One or both of the students to whom Sarah had apologized filed complaints with the university's Office of Student Conduct and Community Standards, and on June 13, Sarah was served with notice that she was being charged with not one, not two, but *five* student conduct charges for her joke – one-and-a-quarter charges *per word*. For making a euphemistic, one-off joke about sex that did not even contain any foul language, Sarah was charged with two violations of her university housing contract, disruption of the university, disorderly conduct, and, of course, harassment. She had two choices: an administrative hearing before an administrator who would unilaterally make a judgment about her case that could not be appealed (but in which she could not be expelled), or a formal hearing in which "all University sanctions [were] possible, including suspension, expulsion, and negative notation on the transcript."

Fortunately, faced with two lousy options, Sarah took a third route: she contacted FIRE. In an 11-page letter sent to University of Oregon president Michael Gottfredson on Aug. 1, 2014, FIRE exhaustively pointed out the absurdity of the situation, the inapplicability of each charge, and the unconstitutionality of a public university punishing a student for a joke. While we at FIRE were certain that Oregon would drop the charges after receiving our letter, the university instead chose to remain silent. On Aug. 26, FIRE issued a national press release about the case. The very next day, the University of Oregon notified Sarah that "[t]he charges against you will be removed and you will not have a student conduct record for this incident," though it did "warn" her about this "behavior" in the future. As with Professor Kipnis, Sarah Emerson's Kafkaesque journey through the Title IX disciplinary system ended only when her inquisitors were publicly exposed and ridiculed for their overreach.

The Feds Concoct a "Blueprint" for Speech Codes across the Nation

Sarah Emerson's absurd and unjust situation can be traced straight back to OCR's Jan. 19, 2001, guidance, which offered a purposely muddled definition of harassment that massively expanded the amount and types of behavior and expression OCR would attempt to regulate. It stated, "Sexual harassment is unwelcome conduct of a sexual nature" and can include "verbal, nonverbal, or physical conduct." (You and I would call "verbal conduct" speech.) This sounds reasonable on first hearing, but it's anything but. Let's take one example OCR and others frequently use: "telling sexual or dirty jokes." Is telling such a joke within earshot of someone who would rather not have heard it sexual harassment? Common sense says no. The law agrees. Simply telling dirty or sexual jokes is a constitutionally protected activity. But in the plain language of OCR's definition, such joke-telling on campus is sexual harassment (although not severe enough to create a "hostile environment").

The genius of redefining constitutionally protected speech as sexual harassment lies in carrying over the impression of moral turpitude that comes from real sexual harassment – like telling your subordinate you'll promote her in exchange for sex – to speech that isn't actually harassment by any sensible definition, such as telling dirty jokes or asking someone on a date who would rather not go out with you. It puts free speech advocates immediately on the defensive by making them either appear to side with "sexual harassment" or spend their time on complicated and often boring wrangling about definitions. It is for this reason that the worst college speech codes have long been enacted under the guise of harassment policies. The 2001 guidance took this deceptive ploy a step further, intentionally putting colleges in a political bind by telling them that they should classify some expression as "sexual harassment" but then should refuse to punish that expression because it did not rise to the level of a "hostile environment."

But it wasn't until 2013 that OCR (joined by the Department of Justice) finally said schools were actually required to use this unconstitutional definition if they wished to be Title IX–compliant. OCR seized on the opportunity of a Title IX settlement with the University of Montana to set forth what it called "a blueprint for colleges and universities throughout the country to protect students from sexual harassment and assault." The University of Montana, which had been embroiled in a nauseating sex scandal involving its football team, was in no real position to protest the fact that the "blueprint" demanded an unconstitutional regime for speech regulation. With the blueprint, OCR and the Department of Justice (DOJ) were tacitly taking the position that both Sarah Emerson and Laura Kipnis are indeed sexual harassers (though not *necessarily* to the extent that they could be punished).

A standard of harassment that required neither intent nor a target struck many people as troublesome.

In fact, the staff members of OCR and DOJ appear to have lost all sense of proportion in their race to use Montana as an opportunity to become a caricature of out-of-control government bureaucrats. Consider this: the resolution agreement with the University of Montana required the school not just to institute mandatory "trainings" to familiarize faculty members with the new, unconstitutional policy and their responsibilities under it, but also to send a list of the names of faculty members who failed or refused to participate *to the Department of Justice.* What in the world did the government plan to do with the list? DOJ never said. As FIRE president Greg Lukianoff put it at the time, with intentionally heavy understatement, "The history of government officials' compiling lists of dissenters is not a happy one." Unsurprisingly, the faculty felt the same way, and the requirement was ultimately dropped.

After FIRE hit the alarm bell as hard as it could and the national media and Congress began to take notice, OCR and DOJ quietly backed away from the blueprint. In a letter to FIRE, OCR head Catherine Lhamon indicated that "the agreement in the Montana case represents the resolution of that particular case and not OCR or DOJ policy," which is pretty much the complete opposite of its earlier declaration that the agreement would be "a blueprint for colleges and universities throughout the country." Yet Lhamon did not see fit to independently inform universities about this change (if she had, perhaps the absurd story of Sarah Emerson would never have happened). This is probably because, like so many government pronunciations on this topic since 2011, it looks like Lhamon's assertion was actually not true. As recently as April 2016, DOJ informed the University of New Mexico that "[u]nwelcome conduct of a sexual nature" – including "verbal conduct" – is sexual harassment "regardless of whether it causes a hostile environment or is quid pro quo."

Thanks to the First Amendment, though, the blueprint is quite susceptible to a legal challenge. Indeed, FIRE brought just such a challenge in January 2016 on behalf of Teresa Buchanan, an education professor at Louisiana State University who was stripped of tenure and fired for her speech under a policy identical to the one promulgated by the federal government under the "blueprint." Her supposed offense was occasionally using profanity and sexual language as a means of teaching her graduate students, in accordance with her observation that today's K–12 classroom is one in which teachers will inevitably face such situations and have to learn to handle them competently. It is FIRE's hope and belief that the federal courts will strike down LSU's regulation as unconstitutional, therefore demonstrating that the "blueprint" itself cannot withstand constitutional scrutiny, despite its strong backing by the federal government.

OCR's Unlawful Assault on Due Process and Fair Procedures

Matching the blueprint for sheer brazenness is OCR's now-infamous Apr. 4, 2011, "Dear Colleague letter" on sexual misconduct ("the DCL"). This letter has changed the course of so many lives, including that of Dave Weber, whose story opened this broadside. Declaring itself to be a "significant guidance document" – in other words, a clarification of the current law and regulations about sexual misconduct on campus – the DCL created out of whole cloth new regulations that all colleges and universities receiving federal funding had to follow.

This positioning of brand-new regulations as simple clarification of the law was no accident. It was intentional deception. OCR labeled the DCL a "significant guidance document" because such "guidance" does not need to go through the official notice-and-comment process that has been mandated since the New Deal era by the Administrative Procedure Act (APA). To understand what happened and why it is so outrageous, a brief history lesson is necessary.

While few have heard of the APA, it's actually critical to the way our country is governed. With the flood of regulations brought in with the New Deal in the 1930s came the concern that administrative agencies would usurp the role of Congress and effectively make laws without any kind of democratic accountability. The APA was Congress's attempt to put some limits on this activity. It requires that new substantive regulations go through a public "notice and comment" period, during which stakeholders are

---

The mandatory sexual harassment trainings in virtually every workplace are the direct result of the adoption of the idea of hostile environment sexual harassment.

---

given a heads-up that a regulation is being considered and are able to submit written comments on those regulations that must be weighed by the regulating agency. Though the agency does not have to agree with comments or make changes because of those comments, the regulators must, at the very least, hear from those it wants to regulate before slapping them with new legal mandates.

Yet the DCL effectively wrote into law two new requirements, to the great surprise of colleges, civil liberties groups, and several U.S. senators, including former secretary of education Lamar Alexander. (In one particularly maddening vignette, OCR managed to tell Senator Alexander in a hearing that the DCL was not legally binding but that OCR expected schools to "comply" with it anyway.) First, it decreed that schools must allow both sides to appeal in a sexual misconduct hearing. In a criminal trial, even for something as minor as a speeding ticket, once you are found not guilty, the process is over. This vital protection against double jeopardy is all that prevents a prosecutor from repeatedly trying to get you convicted of a crime and using up years of your life and all of your money in defense. I had never heard of any college that operated differently until 2011, when OCR decided that accusers in campus cases must be able to appeal even when the accused was found not to have committed the offense. Outrageous though this was, Congress's 2013 reauthorization of the Violence Against Women Act made it the law of the land for now.

The second change, which has proved much more controversial, was the requirement that colleges "must use a preponderance of the evidence standard" (a 50.01 percent certainty of guilt) when determining guilt or innocence in sexual misconduct cases. OCR's contention appears to be that this lowest standard of proof is required by Title IX regulations that mandate that such a hearing be "prompt and equitable," and that a hearing cannot be equitable unless the burden of proof is as close to 50/50 as possible. In contrast, the criminal justice system demands the much higher "beyond a reasonable doubt" standard (a 98–99 percent certainty of guilt), and even civil cases that involve significant reputational damage often require the "clear and convincing evidence" standard (an 80–85 percent level of certainty).

What effect does the preponderance mandate have in the college context? Let's look at some other aspects of the typical college disciplinary system in 2016. First, colleges decide for themselves who will preside over campus hearings and who will serve as jurors. Such panels frequently include college administrators, whose employment prospects may depend in part on their reaching the conclusion most convenient for the college. Some colleges even appoint a single administrator to serve as both judge and jury. Most of the time, neither party to the hearings has a right to active participation of counsel. Cross-examination is limited or even forbidden altogether. There's no guarantee that all the evidence will be shared with both parties – even exculpatory evidence – and the rules of evidence don't apply anyway, with hearsay and other irrelevant "evidence" regularly considered. The parties are usually not placed under oath, and consequences for lying are generally nonexistent. Colleges frequently don't even record the hearing or explain why they came to their decision.

I'd go so far as to say that not a single person at OCR, nor anyone reading this book, would willingly agree to be tried for rape in a system using these rules, run by amateurs, and in which one's guilt or innocence will be determined to a mere coin-toss level of certainty. And the reason neither you nor they would agree to this is precisely because such a system is not, by any stretch of the imagination, just, fair, or equitable. If you require further convincing, imagine a black college student being tried for sexual assault using such rules at the University of Alabama in 1965. Only a madman – or someone utterly blinded by political ideology – would claim that such a system is "equitable." Yet that is precisely the claim OCR makes and that it unlawfully imposes on every college in the country.

There is a remedy for this sort of regulatory abuse under the APA: a lawsuit. While frequently the hardest part of suing the government is proving that you have "standing" to sue – in layman's terms, that the government's actions have specifically damaged you – the students who were found "guilty" of sexual misconduct by campus tribunals under the preponderance standard and who would have been tried under a higher standard before the DCL should have standing to sue. Dave Weber, whose story I opened with, is one of those students.

But Dave isn't interested in suing, and who can blame him? If anything, these "guilty" students have even greater disincentives to sue than do colleges and universities. In the age of Google, nothing is forgotten. Even people ultimately proven innocent of the charges against them, such as the students falsely accused in the infamous Duke lacrosse case, will likely never outrun the notoriety of sexual assault accusations, which are the closest thing to a scarlet letter we have in our society today. It's no wonder, then, that most students are unwilling to challenge OCR in court. Their calculus is simple: What employer, given the choice between two equally qualified candidates, would choose the one who had been found "guilty" of sexual assault by his or her college? What grad school would accept them? Even a student's personal and romantic life is likely to suffer greatly. Who wants to date a possible rapist?

It's the rare student, therefore, who is willing to take on OCR directly and risk his or her name becoming publicly affiliated with the idea of sexual assault. Courts have, rightfully, made this a bit less perilous by frequently allowing students who feel they have been wrongly found guilty on campus to bring lawsuits challenging those findings as "John Doe" plaintiffs – but this is no sure thing, and Doe plaintiffs may be ordered by the court to either proceed under their real name or drop the case. It still requires courage. But such courageous students, though rare, do exist, and, as of June 2016, FIRE has been privileged to find one willing to challenge

OCR's unlawful regulation in court, as well as lawyers willing to take on the tough job of slugging it out with a federal agency in a case where a disgraceful public sliming (as "rape apologists," for instance) of those defending due process is nearly inevitable.

There is another obvious group of plaintiffs who could sue in federal court when OCR promulgates unlawful regulations: the colleges themselves. But OCR has an ace up its sleeve that makes using this remedy extremely difficult – the threat of withdrawing all federal funding from a school. Schools

---

Even students ultimately proven innocent of the charges against them, such as in the infamous Duke lacrosse case, may never outrun the notoriety of sexual assault accusations.

---

live in fear of this power, which so obviously amounts to a death penalty for most schools that it has never been exercised. It doesn't matter much that any school that were to sue would have an excellent chance of winning. Given the slow pace of lawsuits, to do so would require counting on federal bureaucrats who have shown no restraint in violating the law to restrain themselves from retaliating against the school over the years that an APA challenge might take. As a result, it's no surprise that, as of this writing, and after more than 5 years of this patently unlawful regulatory regime, only a single school has been willing to challenge OCR over its obvious APA violation. That school is not the University of Virginia, with its highly publicized rape hoax. It's not the University of Oregon, or even the University of Montana. Out of the more than 4,000 colleges in the U.S., the only school that has proved willing to challenge the DCL in court is the tiny (but bold) Oklahoma Wesleyan University.

Lawsuits can help, but a permanent solution to these problems can only come from a Congress ready to act and a president willing to sign into law reforms of Title IX that will quash OCR's moves to use the law to impose its political will on every school in the country. Although it's unlikely that President Obama, who appointed the OCR heads under whom these abuses took place, would take any specific action to rein in the abuses, it's far from impossible to imagine him signing into law a larger bill that includes reforms to these harmful Title IX interpretations.

Even those unable to get worked up over the fate of students accused of sexual assault need to understand the importance of OCR's regulatory abuse. Perhaps the debate over transgender access to bathrooms will help focus some attention on the problem. In the spring of 2016, the Department of Education decreed that, in the name of Title IX, K–12 public schools must now allow transgender students to use the bathroom and locker room of their choice. (Virtually every parent of K–12 students will likely know about this come the fall.) What they probably don't recognize is that the agency responsible for this decision is OCR and that the mechanism it used to impose this decision was a "Dear Colleague letter" from May 13, 2016, which, even more absurdly than the 2011 letter, it labeled "significant guidance" that "does not add requirements to applicable law." Regardless of your feelings on transgender issues, OCR's argument that a law passed in 1972 requires that students who were born biolog-

Telling dirty jokes is a constitutionally protected activity. But OCR labels it sexual harassment if even a single person is offended.

ically male but who identify as female be allowed to use the girls' locker room at your local public high school – and that this decision is not a change to the law that would, at the very least, require a formal rulemaking process – beggars belief. It is my opinion that the decision to mandate transgender bathrooms in grammar school without going through the normal regulatory progress would simply not have been possible without the supine acquiescence of colleges and universities to the DCL of Apr. 4, 2011.

The substantive due process issues arising from the 2011 DCL are very different from the issue of transgender bathrooms. Yet there is reason for those who care about one issue to follow the other. Culture war considerations frequently warp judicial decisions, especially in an era where courts and judges may act more as mini-legislatures with life tenure than impartial arbiters of the law. But a sufficient number of oxen being gored may have the salutary effect of bringing home to many more people the reality of what can happen when federal agencies like OCR ignore the rule of law in pursuit of social policy. (Apologists for unlawful moves by

President Obama's OCR would be well advised to consider that in 2017, this agency may be under the control of Donald Trump.) Ultimately, there's only one thing that will stop the continued conversion of Title IX from a measure against sex discrimination to an all-purpose justification for the preferred policies of whatever bureaucrat happens to be in power at the time: those who care about free speech, the rule of law, and government accountability must come off the sidelines and vigorously resist these abuses as soon as they happen and regardless of the target — not just when their own interests are finally in the feds' crosshairs.

The author would like to especially thank Jackie Farmer, Greg Lukianoff, Samantha Harris, and Araz Shibley for their help and advice.

First American edition published in 2016 by Encounter Books, an activity of Encounter for Culture and Education, Inc., a nonprofit, tax exempt corporation.
Encounter Books website address: www.encounterbooks.com

Manufactured in the United States and printed on acid-free paper. The paper used in this publication meets the minimum requirements of ANSI/NISO Z39.48–1992 (R 1997) (*Permanence of Paper*).

FIRST AMERICAN EDITION

LIBRARY OF CONGRESS
CATALOGING-IN-PUBLICATION DATA
IS AVAILABLE

Shibley, Robert L.
Twisting title ix / Robert L. Shibley.
pages   cm. — (Encounter broadsides ; 49)
ISBN 978-1-59403-921-8 (pbk. : alk. paper) —
ISBN 978-1-59403-922-5 (ebook)

10 9 8 7 6 5 4 3 2 1